Living
VICTORIOUSLY

STRATEGIES TO EMPOWER WOMEN
WITH A CHRONIC DIAGNOSIS

DORETTA GADSDEN, RN

Strategies to Empower Women with a Chronic Diagnosis

The Information in this book is the writer's experience
and meant to be to read for informative and inspirational
purposes only. By no means is it meant to be taken as a
personal guide.

Revised and republished October 2016 at the sole request
of the author. The publisher is not responsible for any
revisions made after initial publishing.

Please consult your physician for medical advice.
This book is not meant to replace your physician's
advice.

ISBN: 978-0-9861335-6-5

Printed In USA

TABLE OF CONTENTS

"I'm not a victim of the world I see."

- A Course in Miracles

*This book is in dedication to Elizabeth Brown,
my grandmother, who raised me and whose strength
keeps me going today. I love you Mama and I'm so
grateful to have had your love and your example of what
love and perseverance looks like.*

I live my best life daily in honor of you.

Strategies to Empower Women with a Chronic Diagnosis

"You have everything you need inside. Just be still and listen. You will be surprised at what you hear."

Doretta Gadsden

FOREWORD

It is my very great and humble honor to introduce you to the author of the book you are holding in your hands, *Living Victoriously*. Doretta has enough talents and credentials on paper to establish herself as an expert; not only in personally living victoriously but also in helping others get to that vibrant place. She's a registered nurse, a certified professional life coach, and an expert in Emotional Freedom Technique.

If you want to learn how to live victoriously, she's obviously your gal.

But that's not what you need to know about Doretta. You need to know how she wakes up each morning and unwraps the day like a Tiffany box filled with diamonds. When you leave Doretta's presence, you walk away with a highly contagious and infectious dose of incredible energy, and sense that anything is possible, no matter your situation.

When I asked Doretta how in the world she accomplished writing and launching a book between her long hours supporting her patients as a registered nurse, coaching her clients, being the amazing wife, mother, and grandmother that she is, she answered, simply: "Early morning." And then she added, "And I'm waiting for your book, too."

This is Doretta. No excuses, all possibility... a friend, mentor, and coach who holds your vision when you are too tired to carry it yourself.

We all come to the table with our version of circumstances that hold us back from living our dreams. After you read this book, one woman's inspiring story of transforming adversity into triumph, you'll be on fire and motivated to live your dreams as well: to live victoriously.

I hope you turn to Doretta for support when you're ready to do that, because with her help, Women WILL Bloom. Doretta certainly has... but, that's her story to tell.

Relax, pour some tea, and sink into this incredible life she has so generously shared with us in her book, *Living Victoriously*.

~JJ Carolan, MA, CPC, BCBA

INTRODUCTION

This book is for anyone living with a life-changing diagnosis, from Diabetes to Cancer., any diagnosis that has given you pause about how you will move forward with your life.

I am writing this book to share my experiences of living with a life changing diagnosis and the stages I walked through:

- The initial shock and fear
- The steps I took to find a doctor
- My own choices of treatment
- The depression and finding my way out
- My perseverance through numerous hospitalizations

My 22 years as a Registered Nurse as well as my own experience has taught me that with a desire to live our best lives we can find our way.

My hope is that you will gather strength and other tools to walk through this part of your life's journey.

Strategies to Empower Women with a Chronic Diagnosis

"True power comes from cooperation and power."

- Ashanti Proverb

MY DIAGNOSIS

In 1993, I was a new graduate of nursing school, working at Beth Israel Hospital in NYC. I had worked there as a food service attendant, a nurse's aide, and then, later, a Registered Nurse after a position opened on a new AIDS unit was offered to me.

I had cared for many patients living with AIDS, while holding positions as a nurse's aide and food service attendant.

Many of my coworkers treated the patients living with AIDS like they were not human anymore. They were so afraid. I never was. I never wore a mask or felt I could not touch them.

I remember a one male patient of mine. He looked so scared and lonely. I wanted to tell him it was going to be all right, but I knew it would not be. As a nurse's aide it was my responsibility to wrap the bodies after their passing.

Sadly, there were many during that time.

Now I was being offered a position where I felt privileged to have the opportunity to serve; I was so excited to finally have accomplished my goal of becoming a nurse.

After my working there for several weeks, the nursing supervisor announced that all of the new nurses had to be tested for HIV.

My heart started to pound.

You see, ten years prior, in the early eighties, I was an intravenous drug abuser. Most of the people I had been associated with back then were now dead.

They had begun getting sick and then dying from what was then known as "Fever of unknown origin" or New Pneumonia. They were dying so fast.

From Pneumonia?

Or so it seemed.

At this time, they had not yet associated needles with contracting HIV. However, by 1983, I realized whatever they were dying from was connected to the needles we were using. It was the only thing we had in common.

Some people were from upstate, Long Island, some rich, others poor, but what we all had in common was the bowls we rinsed our needles in or the needle we shared.

So, I decided to stop using needles.

Instead, I just snorted the heroin into my nose.

That's why my heart felt like it was going to pound right out of my chest when they announced that we would be tested. I thought, *This is it. I am going to know.*

Definitively.

I decided to tell a coworker I trusted about my history and the concerns I had about possibly being positive for HIV.

Thankfully, she was very supportive.

The man with whom I was living at the time, my dear friend, did not want to know the results. The idea of being tested freaked him out, and he preferred we live in the dark. So I was glad I had my coworker's support.

I went to a clinic that tested anonymously. A man, who was in a twelve step program, provided the intake. He used lots of Narcotics Anonymous slogans, which really annoyed me; I just wanted this over with.

After the testing was complete, he gave me a date to return.

RECOMMITTING TO MY RESOLVE

Over the next two weeks, I just prayed. I looked over my life, at the person I had been and the perseverance it had taken to get me to where I now was.

I remembered moving myself to Minnesota at the suggestion of a woman at the Conifer Park rehabilitation center, to get clean and deal with my demons of incest.

At first, I thought she was crazy asking me to go to Minnesota, a place I had never given a second thought about prior to that conversation. But, she explained that if I did not get to the root of what was running me, the incest experience with my father, the abandonment of the women in my life and their not protecting me, I may not have much of a real future.

I prayed about it and finally agreed with her recommendation.

Everything was put on hold, like the relationship with my partner at the time, my apartment, job, and friends and family. The move took a lot of courage and determination, the intention being to live in a state I had never visited and where I knew no one. But I needed to stop the hell that I had allowed drugs hold me in.

So, I moved to Minnesota, got a room in a local YWCA, and applied for public assistance to gain residency in the state. This was the way I would then be eligible for the excellent rehabilitation services Minnesota was known for.

I was granted an interview with a man at the public assistance office, and he was not quite pleased that I was, as he called it, "a person taking advantage of Minnesota for my personal benefit."

Which was true.

He went on to tell me I needed to go back to New York and find another way to get clean. I left his office feeling defeated and crying; this vision would be an option for me to get clean.

Maybe he had seen my hunger to get my life together, because about a week later he granted me the funds I needed to get into the halfway house. I know that God touched his heart.

I then transferred from the YWCA to Jual Fairbanks halfway house, where I began my healing process, working with counselors and a social worker to overcome the incest and feeling of not being good enough... the feeling that had kept me using drugs to escape the depression.

If you have someone in your life drinking or using drugs, know that something is running them. They are not just inflicting this harm on themselves for fun. They are in hell while using – and an even worse place when they are sober. Find a way to help them.

So, through my stay in Minnesota, I not only got clean, but I also received my GED. It was then that I made the decision to become a registered nurse, so that I could help other people who were hurting as I had been. I knew nursing was a broad field and could help in many areas.

I returned to my life in New York. My partner at the time was very supportive and my job was still there at Beth Israel Medical Center in New York City. If it had not been for that job, I would not have had the resources to go to rehab to meet the counselor who directed me to Minnesota in the first place.

Everything was in divine order.

It was a reminder to me that things are put in our path to assist with our best outcome. Our responsibility is to act. I'm forever grateful I took the invitation to go to Minnesota.

Upon returning to New York, I immediately enrolled in nursing school; I graduated in 1993 from Bronx community college, despite the naysayers' warnings that no one would hire a IV drug abuser or that I would never get a job working with narcotics.

Sometimes, you have to just look at people and bless them, as you leave their space.

So, back to waiting for my test results.

SEARCHING OUT HOPE

Although I was sure I could handle any results, I still prayed for a negative one.

I meditated that morning, as usual; however, in my soul, I knew I was positive. It was like God saying, "You are positive, but you are going to be all right." I remember calling someone to go with me and then going back into meditation, hoping I would get a different message.

The person who went with me to receive my results was the therapist I had hired when I returned to New York to help me continue my healing process. We walked into the center and as soon as I saw the man who was to give me my results, I instantly knew would need someone with more compassion to hold this space for me.

I looked into an office and there was a woman I felt could be fully present for me and not give me some slogan or cliché. So, I told the tester I did not want him to give me my results; instead, I wanted the lady in the loft to give it to me. He said that Susan was the director and did not give results.

I said I would leave without knowing if she would not.

With that, he went into the office to speak with her and through the glass I could see her reaction; she was a little annoyed.

But, still she came out to meet with me.

After ushering me into a private room, Susan barely let me sit down and catch my breath before she blurted out, "You are HIV positive. But, you knew that right?"

Living Victoriously

She had assumed that I knew, because I had checked everything on the high risk list, except for gay, white, and male. Therefore, she had figured I was prepared.

I wasn't.

As she said the words, my mind went somewhere else. It was like she was talking to me through a tunnel. My life, and all that I had accomplished, went flashing through my mind. The friends and patients that I had watched suffer, most of them now dead.

The look on my face obviously made her soften, because she began to provide me with information that would map the course of my walk with AIDS.

As she was speaking, I thought of all that I had been through... Could I do this? Did I have the fight within me to conquer this challenge as I had everything else?

My mind was spinning.

I heard her say that I shouldn't believe everything I'd read about HIV/AIDS, that there were people living full lives with this Diagnosis. I personally did not know of any, but I was willing to believe what she was saying.

There was something about her.

I had personally chosen this woman to give me my results and was now beginning to understand the reason why. Her words were helping me to believe I could possibly make it.

I left the center empowered by this woman, yet feelings of fear and uncertainty were there as well. Susan had given me a lifeline of hope and provided me with a list of places that thought outside the box: support groups and information on alternative treatments. I am so grateful I followed my mind and ask for what I needed in that moment; this woman and the wisdom she offered were a Godsend.

No matter the challenges that I would face living with HIV/AIDS, I felt I would be able to handle it and that I had what it took to live a meaningful life.

Believe me, those thoughts would be put to the test in many ways.

Looking back, I can now understand that I needed to take in what I had just experienced. I was still me but with a challenge that if I could not stand up to, would kill me. If I had chosen to look at this diagnosis through the eyes of fear, I would have sunk into a depression and not come out; I would have been paralyzed from making proactive decisions.

I started my journey by taking one step at a time. The first was allowing myself time to be still. Prayer and meditation were already a place of comfort and guidance, so that is where I continued.

TAKING CONTROL OF MY CHOICES

I returned to work and shared the news with my coworker, Joanne. She was very supportive and took me to a doctor who specialized in infectious diseases, Dr. Michael Mullen at Cabrini Medical Center. I also reached out to the organizations Susan had suggested.

This was the beginning of a journey that would have many ups and downs, many frightening moments, and many days I would not recognize myself while having to make my own decisions, contrary to the advice of others.

This journey would teach me about who I really am and who I am not. My strength and my weaknesses. It would cost me friends and isolate me at times.

And, I will be honest, I would choose to hide away at times, but always reemerge, knowing at bit more about myself.

It was vital to my health that I mentally disassociate from any of the frightening stories around AIDS. Although some thought I was in denial at times, I consistently saw myself having a different walk with this diagnosis than I had witnessed in others.

Many days, it was a challenge. As I have shared, I am a registered nurse and at the time of my diagnosis, I was working on an AIDS unit. I saw patients dying daily. Nevertheless, I still claimed that I would live through this epidemic and have a vibrant life.

WHAT ABOUT YOU?

- What are some of the feelings that have come up for you after hearing your diagnosis?
- What actions can you take?
- What are your beliefs about the diagnosis?
- Where can you get the information that you need?

- In what way can you begin this journey with hope instead of fear?
- How can you take control of this process?

GIFTS TO OFFER YOURSELF

- **JOURNAL:** Write / record your feelings. Journaling is a tool you can use to release whatever it is you are feeling, and it is a great way to track your progress. Sometimes, you may not have a safe person nearby. So, a journal comes in handy for getting feelings out of your body and mind and onto paper. There, you can look at things from another angle. Journals have been life changing for me and many of my clients and patients.

- **CREATE A PLACE** where you can go and be alone, in order to allow yourself time to process your feelings without distractions. Being still is where we get direction for the next right step. Whether you believe in God or not, it is in the quiet spaces that you will hear from your best self, the part of you that knows what is best.

- **TRUST YOUR JOURNEY:** It is important to trust your process. If at all possible, see this diagnosis as a challenge that you can handle with the right self-care. Don't expect to have the same experiences you may have heard others have gone through. Find a way to see yourself beyond your diagnosis and surround yourself with people who will support your positive vision about yourself. If you are not there yet, make up your mind to look for ways to stay upbeat. It will not always be easy. But I know you can do it.

TAKING TIME TO PAUSE

After receiving my diagnosis, I left my therapist and went to the park.

Nature is a place that brings peace and allows me room to be. To think. To relax. It's a place where I feel close to God and it was where I wanted to be.

Needed to be.

Bolstered by my belief in God, I focused on knowing that with God's spirit within me, I had always come through other challenge, even when it took a while to see the end. I was assured that this would be no different.

AIDS was not bigger than God.

This I knew in my soul.

My doubt and concerns came from a lack of belief in myself and my ability... my willingness to fight.

Did I have enough for this?

I had long battled with depression, which caused my thoughts to keep me feeling stuck in places that felt heavy. Thoughts like I wasn't good enough, I wasn't smart enough, and I was definitely unlovable.

My father had molested me and my mother had left me with others to be raised. The fact that she was only fourteen did not take the sting away.

Now this . . .

USING PAUSING AS A TOOL

I had healed from most of the other things. Was I strong enough to fight another battle? Could I use the same tools I did to forgive my parents? The tools were ones I had used to maneuver through the sadness that visited often; I had learned to notice when the sadness approached and to use the tools to stop those feelings at the gate.

I chose to sit with God, asking for guidance and following those directions the best I could. I chose not to allow the fear or images I saw daily to consume me; I refused to believe that would have to be my story or my road.

I reminded myself that in the past, people had told me I would never get off drugs. I did. I went to Minnesota and got clean.

People had told me I would not get through nursing school or be hired because of my past. I did. I had put myself through nursing school and was gainfully employed in my desired career.

These were the same tools I would use now to conquer this situation.

By no means was this going to be easy.

However, my most powerful tool was my ability to pause before acting. It prevented me from making any quick decisions out of fear and what others thought I should do.

Pausing allowed me to take a moment to feel and to know what action to take next. The pause gave me the necessary peace and confidence in myself to make decisions based on relevant research and facts comfortable with me, despite what others thought I should do and what was popular at the time.

Before every decision, I paused, prayed, listened, and then acted. Never did I go against my gut. This was my life, and the same scary diagnosis that was taking my friends and patients quicker than I could take another breath, could have also taken mine.

With God's guidance, protection, and love I had beaten the odds in other areas of my life. I could be the successor in this one as well. Pausing and allowing

God to lead was one of the tools in my treasure chest that kept me here, alive and relatively healthy today. I am really grateful to have this relationship with God. I know I would not have made it without it.

WHAT ABOUT YOU?

Whether you believe in God or not, pausing for a moment to get in touch with how you feel can help you to know what action to take next.

- What ways do you have to get in touch with your innermost feelings and concerns?
- What steps do you take time before a decision to learn what is your best course of action?
- How do you know when you have made the best choice for you?

PAUSING TECHNIQUES TO OFFER YOURSELF

- **Notice Your Breath** and keep your attention as it flows in and out. Take three deep breaths. Notice your body relaxing. Allow yourself to fully relax. Be present. Ask yourself what you need most at this moment. Find a way to care for yourself in the way you need. Your mind cannot focus on fear or anxiety when you focus on your breath. It relaxes you.

- **Say a Favorite Prayer**. Allow yourself to be embodied by it.

- **Do a Mind Dump**. Carry a small journal and when you feeling overwhelmed, fearful or anxious, get alone, breathe, and write. Often when we put our feelings on paper, we feel calmer; we let go of fear and we see more choices.

- **Look at Everything**. Question what is in front of you and recall a time when you overcame something similar.

- **Visualize Yourself at Peace** and handle this moment in the best way possible for you in this moment.

MEETING DR. MULLEN

He swiveled around in his chair and asked "Did you ever think you would die?" At this time, I had been his patient for twenty years. I thought for a moment and realized, No, I hadn't.

I had always believed in Him, in the power of God's love for me and my determination to live beyond the end of this epidemic. It never crossed my mind that I would die. I had things to do. Grandchildren to love. Places to see with my husband.

There were many times I feared not living a full life, not being able to work or have the energy to travel and do things with my family. In those times, I would find peace in my prayer life, readings, and spiritual practice.

It was 1993 when I was first introduced to the man who would become one of my life-lines.

After sharing my news with Joanne and spending some time alone to pause, I went back to the Center.

Joanne had worked with Dr. Mullen for many years and held him in high esteem. He had cared for hundreds of patients since the epidemic began and was the head of Infectious Diseases at Cabrini Medical Center. So, I was impressed when she was able to get me an appointment the same day.

And, I was grateful. I wanted to get the healing process started. I wanted to get everything in order.

Dr. Mullen had a private office not far from Beth Israel. I walked in, registered, and was seen very quickly. He was tall and handsome and very inviting; I was comfortable from the moment I saw him. I could not have known the blessing he would be and the hell he would see me through... several times.

He talked to me, asking about my support system, and laughed with me. I felt very comfortable with him and immediately knew that I was in good hands.

My initial bloodwork was anonymous. Now, Dr. Mullen would have to take more blood in my name. I wish someone had told me to get more life insurance before this, because afterward, I was not able to be insured.

So, I left his office and returned a week later to receive the results of this test.

Although criterion changed as years passed, at this time a person with T-cells below two hundred was considered to have AIDS; mine were 110.

I cried.

Not only did I have HIV, I also had AIDS.

During those moments, he never gave me eye contact, yet he was present in a way I can't explain. I felt afraid and sad, but I sensed he would work it out somehow. I have always felt that no matter what I went through, Dr. Mullen would find a way to fix it.

If he could not, then he would find someone else who could.

I know God sends us angels. They are camped around us, especially at times like these.

Dr. Mullen has been one of mine.

As I write this book, Dr. Mullen has now been my provider for 22 years. He has seen me through some really bad hospitalizations for Pneumonia, TB, Septicemia, and osteomyelitis.

At one time, there was a period when I was unable to go to the hospital where Dr. Mullen practiced, due to a Managed Care misunderstanding. During this time I had to see another doctor until the insurance was corrected.

Even then, he personally counselled the doctors at the other hospital as to how to care for me.

I share this story, because I believe we all deserve a Dr. Mullen. When you are given a life changing diagnosis, you become frightened and foggy. You are not thinking clearly at first. More times than not, you are returning to thoughts of what you have seen others go through; thinking you too will have the same experiences.

It's in those times, you need support from a team of caring people and your doctor is the head of that team.

He or she has to be someone you can trust to respect your opinions and your choices in treatment.

Although Dr. Mullen doesn't always agree when I choose alternative medicine instead of what he has prescribed, he consistently expresses his views, while listening to mine.

When I have gone too far and become out of sorts, we talk and come to a kind of middle ground, which helps me get back on track. In this way, I have learned to marry the two: alternative and traditional medicine.

Over the years, we've worked together, a step at a time, and Dr. Mullen's persepctive has become more open; now he has a couple of alternative books.

WHAT ABOUT YOU?

Choosing a health care team is important when you have been diagnosed with a chronic condition. You want someone who is going to hear your desires and respect them, whether they agree with all your choices or not.

I have a patient who was dismissed from a doctor's service because she would not follow what he had mapped out. That's why it's important that you understand you have the right to care that best suits you, care that you feel at peace with.

GIFTS TO OFFER YOURSELF

Here is a list of things you could consider while choosing a doctor:

- **Be Clear** on what you want.
- **Research the Doctor** before going to him.
- **Find out Their Views** regarding alternative medicine and other forms of healing you may be interested in.

- **Take a List** of your questions and concerns with you.
- **Understand** how you will see them and your access to them.
- **Get a Feeling for the Office Staff**. Are they kind and respectful? How long do you have to wait during most visits?
- **Confirm Your Doctor Specializes in your Diagnosis.** They will know the most up-to-date treatments to discuss with you.
- **Discover other Support Systems** you need to have in place for this to go as smoothly as possible.

CREATING SUPPORT SYSTEMS

At the time of my diagnosis, I had been a part of an incest support group for several months, and I had a therapist as well. I had been clean from drugs for five years, and I had worked hard to heal from my feelings of being damaged, unimportant and unlovable.

I had now reached a place of self-respect.

It would have been more of a challenge had I not had certain support systems in place.

I told my support group immediately. They all embraced and supported me, not treating me any differently.

I also told anyone else that truly meant something to me. I had witnessed people being treated unkindly... even by family members. So, it was important to me that I had their support: that people heard me, that they saw me as the same person I had always been to them, and that they were not afraid of me.

What was most important to me is that my family and close friends saw this as a manageable disease, even though at the time, it was seen as a death sentence.

Living Victoriously

I was blessed. Because, if my closest friends and family ever thought of the diagnosis any other way but manageable, they never showed it.

And, I'm grateful for that. It was critical that I be surrounded by people who would think bigger than an AIDS diagnosis; and if they did not, I removed myself from their presence or limited my time around them.

My therapist at the time was the first to go. She thought we should ruminate about the many dire things that could go wrong; how my future may be one of a woman on disability.

These were not thoughts that I held even at times when my health was most challenged. I always held a vision of health and wellbeing.

She called it denial.

Nevertheless, more than 20 years later, I am still here. If denial got me here... so be it.

Next, I left a twelve step program, because there were people dying daily from AIDS, and the ones living were looking at me, and talking to me, like I would eventually be on the list of those who died.

I was determined to live to see the end of this pandemic. It was like a mantra to me. I would tell my doctor, friends and anyone who would listen, that there has always been a group of people that made it through what seemed like horrible epidemics.

I would be one that made it through this one.

For many years I chose alternative medications. Though I thought Dr. Mullen could walk on water and get me through any health challenge I may face, I did not believe in the medications that were coming out at that time.

Dr. Mullen and some family members did not support this decision, but they respected my right to make it.

It was my life and all I wanted was to be loved and supported in my decisions.

I heard their concerns as well; however, I surrounded myself with people who agreed to disagree with my process, yet still be there for me.

CHOOSING THE RIGHT KIND OF SUPPORT

I began going to a place referred to me by Susan at the clinic where I first received my diagnosis. *Friend in Deed* is an organization which ran support groups for people living with HIV/AIDS and Cancer.

I loved it there.

They were so inviting, loving, and great listeners. I feel like crying in appreciation just thinking about those days spent there.

This was a place where you could just be. They had a large comfortable space with couches, and you could relax and talk to others who were there. You could also participate in the small or large groups that were held there. They had counselors onsite as well.

It was like a big family. Everyone knew each other. It was mostly gay white men, but no one ever treated me differently.

What I really received from my time there was the opportunity to meet people who introduced me to alternative therapies in a deeper way.

This was a place of education on so many levels: meditation, the importance of balance, seeing others thrive and live full lives, and talking about healthy, safe sex.

A haven is what *Friend in Deed* was for me.

Having these support systems in place and people loving, listening, and believing in my process has made a world of difference on my journey to health and wholeness.

WHAT ABOUT YOU?

- Do you have someone you can trust?
- Who can you be honest with about your feelings?
- Who in your life loves you and will just listen?
- Who do you know or can connect with that has experienced this or something similar and can give you positive support?

SUPPORT CHOICES TO OFFER YOURSELF

- Make a list of the people who strengthen you when you are in their presence. These are who you want to surround yourself with right now.
- Limit those who will give you all the negatives about what could happen; instead surround yourself with those who have faith in your plans.

BELIEVING IN YOURSELF

Making decisions for myself during this period was scary at times, and I knew I had to truly learn to believe in myself and act. This was my life.

As I've mentioned before, I respected Dr. Mullen and held him on a pedestal at the time. Nevertheless, I knew he was a traditional doctor with traditional ways of thinking. I wanted to a find my own way.

Directing my own path could be a shaky place when diagnosed with something no one really believes you will live through. Once, I had a relative ask me, "Why are you putting so much into your grandson when you will not live to see the fruit of your efforts?"

This showed me two things: Not only did she feel you had to get something back for giving, but also I became aware of her true belief in my ability to navigate this diagnosis.

In the beginning, my fears were around my ability to work, as well as care for myself and be of use to my grandchildren. *Would I be able to play and travel with them?*

Being disabled was a fate worse than death to me.

Add to that, the fact that I did not have many people who I trusted to take care of me at the time, and I did not want to become a problem to the ones who did love me.

The first change I had to face was my hair falling out. I had lovely locks that I had nurtured and adored for over seven years. After my graduation from nursing school, my hair started thinning and looking weak and unhealthy.

So I cut them off.

My next challenge was when I came down with both TB and Pneumocystis Pneumonia within a three month period. I could not work; one of my worst fears had come upon me.

I became frightened and weak. Mere walking was a challenge. I did not recognize myself. I was thin. I could not breathe. I had no hair. And, I could not work.

As a person who honored alternative medicine, I now had to take over 43 pills a day because you cannot have TB and Pneumonia and talk about Golden Seal and Echinacea.

I began to feel trapped and powerless.

I started using Louise Hay's book *You Can Heal Your Life*, something I had used to help me with my thoughts around the incest. Now I used it for my body. I would talk to my lungs and visualize them getting healthy again. I was aware of the power of thought and seeing oneself bigger than what was happening.

I lived in that book and others like it.

I knew my life would be different. I grew more and more confident that I would continue to realize my dreams. One big desire I had not seen materialize was my being married. I set a dream in motion that I would get married soon.

Everyone thought I was loopy. But I had reference points. I had accomplished most of what I wanted until this point.

I also believed wholeheartedly in my prayers and my belief that nothing is impossible. My believing in myself and God's favor over my life were crucial to my success.

WHAT ABOUT YOU?

- Where do you get your strength?
- What empowers you?
- Who empowers you?
- What are your fears and are they real?
- How do you know they are real?

- How can you put them to the test?

GIFTS TO OFFER YOURSELF
- Study books that give you guidance to learn news ways to cope.
- Choose to live in acceptance of who you are and who you choose to become.
- Strengthen your resolve to realize your deepest dreams.

TAKING CHANCES

Months after my being diagnosed with AIDS, I admitted myself into a mental institution for depression; something I had danced with for most of my life.

During this time, I was not able to work, and I slipped into a state where thoughts of harming myself were more frequent than I would like. Those around me thought it was overkill; that I could manage the sadness. Even the EMS attendant asked me if I was sure I wanted to do this.

They had me with severe mentally ill patients. I just wanted to be with people who were a bit sad like myself. I don't know what I was looking for, but I wouldn't find it there.

I was lucky I got a doctor who kept my status as voluntary, so I could leave whenever I was ready. I stayed a couple of days and followed up with a psychiatrist who I allowed to put me on Prozac.

Antidepressants may work for many, but the two I tried made me feel agitated. They also increased thoughts of unworthiness for being alive.

An example of how the medication worked against me is the day I was at Con Edison paying an electric bill and I was so hyper from the antidepressant that I felt like I was going to take off. I felt racy and full of anxiety.

Afterward, I called the Psychiatrist who let me know I could get off the medication whenever I chose.

So, I did and searched for other ways to handle my mood swings. One was exercise. I realized that moving my body daily lifted my mood, and in turn I would have the energy and mental strength to do other things that were also life affirming, one right step at a time.

Another discovery was I needed to eliminate sugar from my diet. Sugar exacerbated my sadness and made me tired. This became a vicious cycle: I'd eat sweets, get tired, and sleep, or not do all that I had planned. So I had to decide whether I wanted to feed my taste buds or have energy and be productive. Most times I went for the latter.

Not perfectly, but in moderation.

In this manner, I continued to care for myself in ways that felt right to me.

Another instance was that I had been in a twelve year relationship I needed to leave. This was one of those unpopular moves that no one in my life understood.

Honoring My Choices

This person had been good to me. He was there to guide me off drugs; he helped me go through nursing school. He was just an overall good person.

What no one could see was that I wasn't happy. The one thing that I wanted most in life at that time was to be married. He would give me the world, but not that.

I wanted to travel; he would not. I wanted to have someone to belly laugh with. I wanted to know life on a whole new level, and I was willing to risk being alone to find this. I would not stay in a relationship because it was something familiar.

For me, it was time to go.

With everyone looking at me oddly, I asked him to leave. And I got on with my life: finding myself without him, seeing who I was on my own.

Several years later, after I traveled with friends and discovered more of my own strength and independence, I found someone and at the writing of this book I have been married sixteen years. We've been together eighteen.

And yes, I get daily belly laughs.

WHAT ABOUT YOU?

- What are some ideas you want to try?
- What is your gut telling you to choose?
- How can you make choices despite others not agreeing with you?
- What actions do you need to take to make your dreams a reality?

GIFTS TO OFFER YOURSELF

- **Identify Pressures** others put on you to keep things as they are. Make sure your choices are for YOU and not just to please someone else.
- **Notice what feels wrong** and figure out ways to make it feel right; then make the necessary changes.

- **Be willing to change your mind**. New information, new experiences, and new perspectives can cause you to rethink old choices. Don't feel that you have to continue to commit to what you previously thought best.

- **Form your best relationship with yourself first**. Until you are fully comfortable living your own life, you cannot be fully happy. Make the choices that feel right for YOU.

FORGIVING MY SHORTCOMINGS

I had come to see myself as different, yet in a positive way. I saw my strength and determination. I saw my ability to walk through fear and get the things I needed accomplished.

Yes, I have changed.

I am more willing and able to create what I want, and I have more courage in taking risks.

Having grown to accept that my choices have created some unwanted situations, I no longer allow myself to sit with guilt, shame, and depression for very long. Feelings that were once part of my life still show up; however, I don't entertain them any longer.

My inability to care for my children had been a source of shame and hurt. I watched my daughters go through things that I wanted to protect them from, but because of my own hurt and open wounds, I was ill-prepared.

I would not to forget the son I gave up for adoption. Thus, the word "Mother" would make my stomach turn for many years.

Living Victoriously

I wore shame like a coat I could not free myself from. For so long I wanted a do over.

I had my eldest daughter when I was sixteen; her paternal grandmother raised her. My youngest daughter was put in foster care when my addiction got out of hand and later adopted openly, giving me the opportunity to see her after some time had passed.

If I had known a better way to cope with my feelings of hopelessness and shame, I'd have better managed living and dealing with the feeling of abandonment instead of sinking into deep depression and thoughts of killing myself.

However, heroin seemed to make everything feel normal. It stopped the pain, but it cost me healthy relationships with my children. That is one of my biggest lessons and regrets.

Some people say they have no regrets. I'm happy for them. The loss of raising my children is mine. Do I lose sleep? No. I have forgiven myself, but I still look at my daughter and think *what if?*

So, today I am the person I can be to my children. It has taken years for me to move into forgiving myself. My eldest daughter and I are trying to build a relationship one text at a time and I have peace with that.

My youngest is working through her own issues, and I have a loving relationship with her and my beautiful grandchildren. She has blessed me with a chance to mother in a whole new way.

Today I accept all my choices and allow others theirs. We are all doing the best we can with what we have, no more, no less.

Today I love and respect myself and my journey.

WHAT ABOUT YOU?

- What do you need to forgive yourself for?
- Are you willing to forgive yourself?
- What steps can you take to start your forgiving process?
- How can you allow others their choices as well?
- What are some of your strengths?
- How can you use them now?

GIFTS TO OFFER YOURSELF

- **Accept the choices that created unwanted situations**, but stop allowing yourself to sit with guilt, shame, and depression.

- **See the life you want to create** and identify the choices that sidetracked you. Encourage yourself to leave the old choices behind and take the new risks that will help you get where you'd rather be.

- **Consider any regrets you have**. Realistically choose new ways to approach the situation so that you will achieve a better future outcome in ways that you still can.

MY RELATIONSHIP WITH GOD

I have believed in God since I was little.

Of course, my definition then was a bit different than now. While growing up, He was a man in the sky who punished you if you did something wrong and only loved you when you were good.

As I grew and searched, my belief broadened and softened. To be honest, in my heart, I did not believe the hell and fire sermon too much anyway. It just did not sit right in my gut, and as I lived with more presence, I came to know a more loving, supportive, protective God who would not allow me to suffer so much, unless I chose to.

When I was in my grips of my addiction, I would carry a small King James Bible. I can see its green cover as if it were in my hand right now. It was my strength. It gave me courage. It served as my protection.

For some reason, I believed I would be alright walking the streets at three in the morning, or when I was sick and lost half of my body weight, or when I thought I would really lose all my rights to my youngest daughter.

It was like, all I had to do was get still, be quiet, and listen. The spirit of God that lives within me would always give me the right direction.

Always.

Like when I received a letter informing me that all my parental rights regarding my youngest daughter were going to be taken in a couple of days because I had not pulled my life together in time. I received direction as I was crying; instructing me to write a letter to my daughter's adoptive mother.

I did.

And, I told her what my daughter meant to me. In spite of how things looked, she was the one thing that kept me reaching and wanting to get off drugs. I invited her to put herself in my shoes. How would she feel if she lost her children? I felt I had nothing but her and they were now going to take her as well.

Thankfully, she heard me and elected to make the adoption open, eventually becoming one of my closest confidants.

Another instance was the night I was sitting in a shooting gallery, just sitting. And I received the thought that I was just passing through... that this and all my other seeming painful experiences would be a pathway for others. I chuckled, but in my gut, I believed I would be shown how to come through this very dark place.

Several weeks later, I met a friend who God used to transform my life. This friend loved me and helped me get stable and become the nurse I am today.

My little green bible and the Psalms I read opened parts of me that gave me hope. I found the strength to put one foot in front of the other, to move through pain and fear, to search for forgiveness like it was gold.

My prayer life led me to other sources of God as well. I began to see the spirit of God everywhere.

Unity church was where I found a way to truly learn and worship the God spirit that lives within all of us. The teaching was nonjudgmental. My gay friends were not going to hell. My power lay within a God who lives within me, not in the clouds.

So, through all my peaks and valleys, I have always known I had the spirit of God within me, guiding, protecting, and loving me.

Later, during one of my physical challenges, I read about the prognosis and according to the medical book, it seemed bleak. But I knew something more: I knew that the spirit of God is bigger than any diagnosis; I knew that although I was experiencing indescribable pain, I believed it would pass.

And it did.

Today I am grateful to have a relationship with a God that is unshakable. I know that as I breathe, that spirit of God is within me. That is why I am conscious of meditating and living in the moment. That is where God is: right here, right now.

The God I have come to know and respect directs us, loves us through our scary moments, and is ever present.

THE UNITY PRAYER OF PROTECTION

The Light of God surrounds us
The Love of God enfolds us
The Power of God protects us and
The Presence of God watches over us.
Wherever we are God is and all is well.

WHAT ABOUT YOU?

- What does God mean to you?
- How can you use a power greater than yourself to support you now?

- How can you be bigger than this diagnosis?

GIFTS TO OFFER YOURSELF
- Write: If God could help, what do you need right now?
- What would you want to say to God about this diagnosis? Write, Draw, or Speak it into a recorder.

LISTENING AND BELIEVING

My comfort with being alone has made my healing process move more easily. I love the quiet of the mornings. I feel like it is me and God, which His spirit is speaking through me.

The many hospital stays were only survived by my ability to listen to God's prompting, regardless of what the situation looked like.

For me, taking time to listen and trusting enough to act has moved me to where I am today.

If I had doubted that I would make it out of the shooting galleries and not acted on God's directions, I would still be there or dead. If I had not written the letter to my daughter's adopted mother, our relationship would not have shifted. If I believed everything the medical books said about my diagnoses instead of listening and believing what God was saying, I would not have gotten out of bed many days.

Life would have seemed hopeless.

My quiet time is when hope is at its best: I feel fully alive, and I am present with God with no other judgments or opinions to cloud my understanding.

People in my life can have a lot to say. But they were not walking in my shoes.

It has been important to learn to trust myself.

Despite watching others go through similar diagnosis, I had to create a thought pattern that I was an individual and my process was my own, unlike any other.

That thought pattern has kept me going.

One move at a time.

WHAT ABOUT YOU?

- What are some of your beliefs about yourself?
- Who are you listening to?
- Is it supporting you in your forward progress?

GIFTS TO OFFER YOURSELF

- Write your ideas about how you can create and benefit from quiet time now and always.

AIDS, COPD, and DEPRESSION

AIDS, COPD, and depression have been three of my biggest health and life challenges. They have altered the way I see myself, the world, my relationship with God, and faith.

They made me value how I use my time and have each given me a new way of both seeing and experiencing life.

Although the diagnoses came at different times in my life, they were often felt all at once.

DEPRESSION

I have experienced depression since adolescence; I have felt alone, isolated, unloved, and so misunderstood. Being molested by my father just added to my sense of not feeling important.

No one seemed to believe me, which hurt me so much. Why would I make something like that up about a father that I adored? I could not understand the women in my family not supporting and protecting me.

I know my father wielded power, but I wanted them, my grandmother especially, to speak up and protect me.

My stepmother was quite indifferent to me. I never expected her to do anything. She acted like she hated me and I did not understand that. As an adult I realized she possibly knew and maybe was jealous or felt powerless herself.

Whatever the reason, these women made me feel so unsafe in the world and very sad. I would befriend anyone who would show me kindness. I was starving for love and attention; not getting it from the ones I would have expected. The depression was like a heavy blanket over me, something I carried and could not shake off. Even good things would be overshadowed by this cloud.

Around the age of twelve, I began hanging out with older people who used drugs, methadone to be specific.

That would numb the sadness quickly.

So, for most of my life, I grasped for peace of mind and spirit, a sense of belonging and of being loved. It was that hunger that kept me using drugs for so long.

I kept searching: The Bible. *A Course in Miracles*. Prayer. Groups. Journaling. Forgiveness. I checked out whatever I heard held the promise of freedom from depression and feeling so lost.

This is what finally worked for me:

- **My Prayer Life:** My walk with God. I have searched for God in many places and He has always shown up. The Bible has not been the only place the Spirit of God has led me. My forgiveness walk came from *A Course in Miracles;* I could not get there via the Bible. The spirit of God is in many places. This I know for sure.

- **Exercise:** If I move my body, I feel better. I don't do a lot; some days, if I do a few yoga postures, I'm good. It's just getting my endorphins up. Walking is a blessing for me as well.

- **Watching My Sugar Intake**. Sugar in all her forms is a challenge. I have to watch bread, pasta, rice, or anything that turns into sugar. This allows me to function at my best and changes my mood. Quickly.

- **Being Ok With My Own Accomplishments:** In other words, I'm careful to not compare myself to another person's outside.

- **Journaling:** Writing helps me look at my surroundings and list the things I'm grateful for, which helps me feel good about my life.

- **Remembering Feelings Will Pass.** And things always work out for my best. It may not be exactly how I want it, but it will be ok. That has been my experience.

So, this is how I keep depression at bay in my life today. It shows up at times, but I don't sit and entertain it as I used to. I know I have tools and choices.

And, I use them.

Depression is paralyzing and it has cost me too many years of my life, stealing more time than AIDS and COPD combined.

This is why I keep watch for the time I give it when it appears.

AIDS

My walk with AIDS has been very adventurous, to say the least. I was hospitalized more than twenty times in the late 1990's and early 2000's.

Most of my hospitalization had to do with my preference for alternative medicine over traditional medication, as well as my working long stressful hours with four to ten T-cells, thinking I could pray my way in staying healthy.

I could not.

So, after not being able to walk home from a patient's home in 2001, I have been blending traditional and alternative healing practices.

I also use Visualization and Tapping/ Emotional Freedom Techniques (EFT). When I was first diagnosed, I saw AIDS as this energy that lived inside me, and I knew I needed to make peace with it until I could find a way to release it. Heal it.

I did not choose to see it as a war I was fighting or even as something that would kill me, even though that is what I saw happening to my patients and many associates and friends. If I saw it as a war or something that would kill me, I would have been put on the defensive, causing me to become afraid, which only makes me freeze. I did not need that.

Instead, I made up meditations and visualizations where I saw the virus as children with ADHD, who were lost on my island, wreaking havoc. Their boat had been shipwrecked and they just needed to get back home, where they could relax.

I would visualize myself talking to the virus saying, "I am going to get you back home; you just need to stay calm." I would see the boat I had provided for them and usher a little off each day. At the same time, I would visualize healthy T-cells popping up like popcorn and energizing my body.

One day, I was feeling really tired and sad. So, I wrote a poem about the virus.

"Temporary Resident"

You eased in, quietly, slowly at first not really disturbing

Slowly, imbedding yourself in my very being

Still, I was unaware. Slowly, as is your pattern,

You made yourself known. First, with weakness and other daily annoyances,

Never apologizing for the damage you caused. The space and time you occupied.

I ask this, until I find a way to release you, can you and I peacefully co – exist? 10/14/1999

It was important for me to put the visualization into a context that made sense to and for me.

Another way I deal with the virus is to use EFT; although there are no needles used, EFT is best described as acupuncture for the emotions. This method is founded on the belief that unwanted feelings and negative emotions can create a block in our system, allowing the negative feelings and emotions to remain trapped within us.

By tapping on certain pressure points, we are able to release physical pain and unblock old patterns that have been holding us back.

As one who has danced with depression for some time, I use tapping whenever thoughts resurface about my not being good enough, or when I feel overwhelmed. It has even kept me from saying and doing things I would have to apologize for later.

It may sound a bit off the beaten path, but it works for me. I believe we have the power within to heal ourselves. We just have to listen, be creative, and implement what works for us, not what works for everyone else.

COPD (Chronic Obstructive Pulmonary Disease)

I have to be honest. If I was given a choice to trade in one of my diagnoses, this is the one I would give back. It affects your very basic life force: your breath. I used to smoke two packs of cigarettes a day when I did drugs. And I have caused a bit of damage to my lungs.

This is the diagnosis that is most apparent in my life. It affects where I go, how I move, what I decide to eat. Examples:

- Fragrances: I think twice before I go somewhere that is heavy in fragrances; certain ones could cause me to become short of breath or start a cold. I so dislike having to avoid aromas I enjoy, but this is a part of my life right now.
- Foods: I love dairy foods such as milk, butter, and cheese, but I have to limit them and really should eliminate them completely. However,

being transparent, I cheat at times when I know I'm going to be home and can cough all I want. One day, I may be able to tell you I'm prefect in this area. Not today.

- Smoke: I'm a visiting nurse, as well as a speaker and life coach, and I have to be mindful of the homes I go into. I always ask the patients if they smoke. If they do, I ask them to stop at least a half hour before I arrive. I have never had anyone have an issue with it.

I have also been fortunate with none of these patients requesting another nurse, due to my going into coughing fits for a couple seconds. Instead of saying I have COPD and explaining it, I just say I have Asthma. Nine times out of ten, they have a family story of someone who has experienced Asthma.

For the COPD patients I'm close to, I just tell them I live with the same diagnosis as they do. They see me live a relatively healthy life, always upbeat and breathing without a device. I use this as a teachable moment to tell them about diet, breathing exercises, and pacing their activities, as well as about avoiding environmental irritants such as heavy perfumes, certain cleaning supplies, and air fresheners.

For a long time, I did not publicly speak or coach because of the chance I might start coughing. Then, several people suggested I incorporate it into my workshop, which is titled Living Well with a Chronic Diagnoses, as well as teaching EFT.

So I did. And, my workshop has consistent members.

We can sit in a corner and feel sorry for ourselves or we can ask God / our Higher Self how to use what is in our lives to best serve ourselves and others.

These have been my challenges and still are some days. They are a part of my life; however, I don't allow them to define who I am or what I'm capable of accomplishing.

Nothing can stop me until God is finished using me to serve.

WHAT ABOUT YOU?
- How do you see your life now?
- How can you make it what you want it to be?

- What stories can you create that would lessen the stress or fear around your diagnosis?
- How can you use it to bless others and yourself in the process?

GIFTS TO OFFER YOURSELF

- Create a story around your diagnosis that empowers you and others.
- Create a visualization that you can meditate on daily.

MY CIRCLE OF INSPIRATION

As I mentioned earlier, having a support system is key to your being able to deal with many of the challenges you will face. I have been blessed with not one, not two, but at least three people in my life who have served as a source of inspiration for me: my husband, my teacher, and my grandson.

GLENN: MY HUSBAND

"My husband."

Just saying those words brings a smile to my face. He has been such a solid place for me through many times of testing. He has been a coach with some amazing life-provoking questions I needed at moments when I forgot who I was. He has been a nudge at times when I needed a push in the right direction. And always, he offered me a belly laugh.

I met my husband by answering an ad in the Personal section of a magazine we both read. His ad was three lines, short and friendly. I had an ad in the same section he says was too long and very conditional. He felt he had only a few of the many things I was asking for, so he just did not answer.

His ad was the only one I reached out to.

Eighteen years later, here we are. He is a soft spot for me when I need that. But more than anything, he never lets me wallow too long when I have felt sick.

It was almost like he had a timer.

He would remind me about what we both know about healing, affirming, movement, and body work.

He has been a very present source of my joy.

We have a loving, blended family, with his three and my two daughters. Together, we have ten grandchildren and four great-grandchildren.

Most of my life, I never felt like I belonged anywhere. My dream was to build a loving family that I could feel a part of. I wanted our home to be the place everyone came for Christmas and Thanksgiving.

Together, we have created that.

Through my many hospitalizations, I always knew I had someone in my corner, even if no one else was there.

He has never let me down.

MAGGIE: SEEDS THAT KEEP GIVING

When I was 13 years old, and after the incest was discovered, I was sent away to a place called Holy Cross. It was a place for children who were acting up or runaway, which I had been. There, I felt even more isolated and alone.

It was during this time that I did not have a voice of my own or did not know it; I was the opposite of who I am today. Almost invisible.

At least that is how I felt.

Maggie was the counselor assigned to me. I can see my first meeting with her as if it were today. She had the most beautiful blue eyes, her thick brown hair rested just below her shoulder blades, and she had an ease with her walk, a freedom, so to speak.

I was standing in the hallway at my room door, and she walked up to me and introduced herself.

I just looked at her and said ok. I did not know what to expect. She seemed so nice and very interested in getting to know me.

In my mind, she was white, and I had been raised by a militant father who was, along with being a child molester, a Black Panther. If you don't know their history, they did not speak well of whites.

So, now I was in front of this woman, who says she wants to get to know me.

I stay open.

No one else was around to care.

During the next two years, the love and support Maggie gave me and the things I was exposed to, planted a seed that would later give me the strength and vision to rise up out of some very dark places.

Maggie showed me kindness and unconditional love from a race of people I had been taught to mistrust. She taught me that I was not where I came from or what had happened to me.

She instilled in me that I was bigger than any act that had been put upon me.

In her presence, I flourished. I believed in myself and my ability to become something bigger than that which I had come from.

I felt loved and seen, something I had not experienced at home. My family's first priority was keeping my father out of prison, something my grandmother later apologized for before she passed. I must say I loved her dearly and never had any hard feelings toward her.

One day, my father came to visit with his wife. After they left, I had somewhat of a nervous breakdown. I started crying and they could not control me.

At one point, Maggie kept asking me if I knew what I was saying. I remember her asking but not what was coming out of my mouth.

They had me taken to the infirmary where I was given a shot of Thorazine, an antipsychotic that made it difficult for one to think. I guess they did not have valium or something else on hand.

My father was never invited back. Maggie was very supportive and I believe she was instrumental in my being taken off the Thorazine within a couple of days.

Maggie left Holy Cross after I was there for two years. She would come get me and take me to her home with her daughter, Danielle.

Through this relationship, I was able to see what was possible to build for myself, that I could create anything I wanted, if I just believed in myself.

Before Maggie, I did not think I was lovable.

Because of her, I am now able to allow myself to believe in the face of unbelief; I have my own voice.

I know that I matter.

Wherever you are Maggie... Thank You.

MARQUIS: THE FOCUS THAT SAVED ME

I believe when faced with any life changing diagnosis, after we decide our healthcare needs, teams, treatment, and support systems, it is vital to have a purpose bigger than you and your diagnosis.

My grandson Marquis was mine.

He was my first born grandson and I adored him. We were very close.

One day, he and my daughter came to visit. He walked into my home and did not recognize me; I had just had a bad case of Shingles that left the right side of my face scarred and an eye partially closed.

On top of that, it had shifted or morphed into Post-Herpetic Neuralgia, something I would not wish on anyone. The intermittent pain was debilitating and immobilizing and there was nothing I could do until it passed, which usually only took several seconds, though it seemed like an hour.

Marquis walked in looking for his Nana and saw me instead. He could not wrap his mind around my transformation. I was a healthy woman several weeks ago and now this. Where was his Nana? My voice was the same, but my appearance frightened him.

It cut me like a knife.

After this, my daughter helped me through several of the excruciating headaches that lasted 15 – 20 seconds but felt like fire running through my brain.

When they left, I asked God to please help me get through this so I could be present for Marquis. I had seen him come into this world. I was there when he was born. He had become my life and now he did not recognize me.

Oh, no, I could not leave him like this.

I believe my prayers and my love for Marquis, my belief that he needed me to live a great life, kept me healthy until he was an adult.

He was my reason for continuing to search for ways to remain healthy, a motivation indeed.

If I felt like something was going wrong with my body, I would get to praying, juicing, and anything else in my treasure chest that kept me healthy and on point to care for him.

It is amazing that loving someone else can give you the strength to accomplish what seemed impossible. No longer did I make room for illness to come and weaken me.

That would have taken away from Marquis.

My love for him has been a blessing. It was my focus. A focus that changed the course of my thoughts and what I allowed myself to entertain as far as my health.

WHAT ABOUT YOU?

- Who are those within your circle of inspiration?
- How do they motivate and encourage you to come through this challenge?
- How can you be a source of inspiration for yourself?

GIFTS TO OFFER YOURSELF

- Write or draw about your circle of inspiration or whatever inspires you.

MY STORY, MY BLESSING

Well, this has been my story of living with chronic diagnoses. My prayer is that my story has blessed you in some way. Please feel free to contact me with any questions on coaching, speaker engagement or my retreats.

Be blessed and always be encouraged with the knowledge that you are bigger than any diagnosis.

MY TREASURE CHEST

- The Bible: A book of inspirational stories on how to live life.
- *You Can Heal Your Life* by Louise Hay: A book on healing your mind and body.
- *A Course in Miracles* by Dr. Helen Schucman: A Book channeled through a woman on looking at life differently.
- EFT – Emotional Freedom Technique: A way to use your finger tips to assist with healing.
- *Your Word is Your Wand* by Florence Scovel Shinn: A book teaching the power of your words and thoughts.
- *The Work* by Byron Katie: Four questions and a turnaround that invites you to look at all your stressful thoughts.
- *The Four Agreements* by Don Miguel Ruiz: A book on four agreements that, if practiced, could change your life.

Strategies to Empower Women with a Chronic Diagnosis

I can do all things through God who strengthens me.

Philippians 4:13

ABOUT THE AUTHOR

Doretta Gadsden is a Registered Nurse for the past twenty-two years and a certified life coach for four.

Doretta has lived with several life changing diagnoses herself and knows the fear and uncertainty that accompanies this. She has a passion for holding space for each woman to be educated and empowered to make life affirming choices around her health.

Her "Your Life in Bloom" Program is a six week program where she supports you in discovering what is needed for you to move forward in your life and take control of your health care.

Visit her at www.womenwillbloom.com
info@womenwillbloom.com
929-265-0288

PUBLISHER:
Angel B. Inspired Inc.
P.O. Box 49647
Greensboro, NC 27419
(704) 978-8679
www.angelbarrino.com
www.angelbinspired.com
angelbinspired@gmail.com

Editing/ Interior / Cover Design:
DHBonner Virtual Solutions LLC
www.dhbonner.net

After Publication Revisions/Final Proofing/Editing:
Kae Bender, EverydayEditing.com

www.ingramcontent.com/pod-product-compliance
Lightning Source LLC
Chambersburg PA
CBHW070108070426
42448CB00038B/2217